SUNRISE

Some more books of White Eagle's teaching

SUNRISE

WHITE EAGLE

IN LOVE THERE IS NO SEPARATION

THE WHITE EAGLE PUBLISHING TRUST
NEW LANDS · LISS · HAMPSHIRE · ENGLAND
www.whiteaglepublishing.org

First published October 1958
Second edition November 2001
Second impression, with illustrations added, January 2003

Line drawings by Rosemary Young

© Copyright,
The White Eagle Publishing Trust, 1958, 2001
ISBN 0-85487-114-4

British Library Cataloguing-in-Publication Data
A catalogue record for this book
is available from the British Library

Set in 12pt auto-leaded Baskerville
and printed and bound in Great Britain
at the University Press, Cambridge

CONTENTS

Preface to the Second Edition

Jenny Dent

THE FIRST EDITION of SUNRISE was published in 1958. It contained quite a lengthy introduction by Grace Cooke which among other things introduced the gift which she there called 'second sight'. In her own life having this gift enabled her to contact the inner spiritual worlds, and thus to provide deep comfort to the bereaved. It was a gift she possessed independently of being the channel for the teacher White Eagle, whose name is now recognized all over the world, and it was one which manifested long before her subsequent work in founding the religious charity known as The White Eagle Lodge. However, it is White Eagle as teacher who most interests us in this book. His name is partly symbolic, although it does denote a particular personality. To quote from the most recent White Eagle book THE LIGHT BRINGER:

7

'We come to you under the name of White Eagle, but would explain that we speak for a large company of shining beings, angels and illumined souls of men and women who are sometimes referred to as the Star Brotherhood. We have the name of White Eagle because our message is the message of John, the beloved of the Lord Jesus. John is the lightbringer; White Eagle is a humble servant, but the symbol of the white eagle is one used by John the Beloved, the teacher of the new age of Aquarius. This light is gradually being born upon your earth plane.'

During this new age of Aquarius, I should like to suggest, greater understanding will dawn of the inner spiritual worlds which interpenetrate the physical world. As this understanding grows, more people will be able to become aware for themselves of the continuing life after physical death of their loved ones. An important aspect of the work of the White Eagle Lodge is to help people do precisely this: to obtain for themselves a conviction about life in another world and to develop a real picture of it.

Grace Cooke was my grandmother, and I believe that when she wrote her introduction to SUNRISE, people were not so aware of their opportunity to make the inner contact for themselves. Since that time, understanding of meditation and inner communion has developed a great deal and is part of the impulse of the new Aquarian age. White Eagle has stressed this as the way to make the inner contact just described, actually in preference to the use of mediumship, however good that may be, because it is a surer way and leads to the unfolding of other spiritual gifts in the self. However, when going through bereavement everyone is in need of comfort, reassurance and help. It is not at all easy in a state of loss and grief to make one's own contact, and any help is of great value and reassurance. Minesta (as she was known to so many) knew this, and it was a very meaningful part of her work to give human comfort to those who were suffering loss. Although she was a great advocate of meditation and helping people make their own inner contact as described, she would always do her best to give help to anyone in need.

I was fortunate to be working very closely with Minesta as personal assistant and secretary from the mid-sixties through to the time in the mix-seventies when illness prevented her continuing this work. I particularly remember one occasion when parents wrote to her in great distress about the loss of their daughter in a drowning accident. As she tuned in and, as it were, built the bridge to the other world through her own psychic gifts, she truly brought the child into the room where we sat. I became very aware of this lovely smiling girl with curly fair hair. The parents had not described her at all to my grandmother, but she described this little girl to them in the letter we wrote. Subsequently they replied that everything was absolutely true and had brought them very great comfort indeed.

Minesta was also called by White Eagle 'Bright-Eyes', a most appropriate name. I can remember the way in which just looking into her eyes gave a feeling of another dimension—one knew she was seeing into the inner world and seeing them with great clarity. On a number of occasions I was fortunate to experience the beautiful way in which she was able to give people she was with true and evidential messages from loved ones who had passed on.

In her original introduction to SUNRISE, Minesta gave an account of one such instance, when she was able to give help to a grieving widow. She wrote of that person's initial condition thus:

'Her mind constantly dwelt upon various episodes of his last illness, and she could neither believe nor accept that the time had truly come for her husband to pass on into wider fields of service in a happier state of life. At our first meeting she was inconsolable and little could be done to help her, so densely was she enveloped by grief and self-pity. However, she was told that by her attitude of mind she was preventing any consolation coming to her from the spirit of her husband, because her darkness was impenetrable by the subtler ether which is a component substance of the spirit world. Nor is this unusual in bereavement;

self-pitying and grief-laden thoughts, which are usually so prevalent at a death, not only bring despair to the mourner but also nullify any efforts to assure them that all is well; that their loved ones are happier and healthier in their new state of life than ever before. As I explained these things to this poor widow, she gradually became less distraught, and the mists surrounding her began to dissolve. Then, quite near her, could be seen the spirit of her husband. He presently convinced her of his reality by giving her many details about their life together, and by his mode of speech, thought and mannerisms proved his presence, so that she eventually believed that he was still alive and was much comforted. His messages are too personal to be repeated, but she wrote in a letter to me:

"'Tonight I dreamed of my husband, and he took hold of my hand and pressed it in a sympathetic way—I could feel it *before* I woke up. That was an immensely comforting dream, because he pressed my hand so kindly and lovingly…. On another occasion I went to sleep while writing a letter, and dreamt of my husband saying that he had sent six messages to me. Actually I have only received two of them clearly." But she wrote again later: "I have been fortunate enough again to dream of my husband several times, and each time I saw him quite distinctly. All this makes me long more than ever for another chance of showing more sympathy and kindness.'"

Minesta then explained further about the way in which contact can be made between the two worlds and how friends can help in this process.

'Contact between the living and the dead is, I believe, first established on some higher etheric level. Moreover, I am convinced that in the spirit world an accurate and detailed organisation exists whereby sympathetically-attuned friends and someone they have lost can be brought into contact. This means that when people are ready, and can open their minds to the possibility of such communication, there are those in the beyond appointed for this particular service of linking mutual friends separated by death. Communication can then be established through these helpers' knowledge of the spiritual laws of attunement, which cannot be fully understood or appreciated by the unenlightened.'

Minesta, Grace Cooke, most truly was able to build a bridge of light between the two worlds. This work did not end after her passing in September 1979. Indeed, it seemed to become even more significant, because she was newly released from the heavier conditions of the physical world, and in the finer vibration of the spiritual one she had a very special way of being able to impress her presence quite easily upon those still in the physical, and bring their loved ones with her. I first experienced her presence just two weeks after her passing. I was in New Lands garden when I felt her sit beside me. I knew it was she, even before I had 'seen' her new body of light. It's interesting how one knows and feels the vibration of someone, and knows who they are through that vibration rather than an actual 'seeing'. But when I did open my inner eyes, I saw that she was in a young body with long dark hair, not in the tired body that she had had before her passing. When I called her 'Nanna', which was my childhood name for her, she said, 'Oh no, don't call me that: call me Minesta. I am your sister Minesta'. And I could see that she was in fact wearing the young body from the Mayan life when I was her sister in the Andes.

Loved ones can take on the 'dress' or body of previous lives, although obviously normally they would appear in a way that they can be recognized. When my mother, Joan Hodgson, passed on in 1995, it was as though she inherited more distinctly than in life my grandmother's role of making the bridge and bringing comfort to those who were grieving. There definitely is some significance in the special way those who are newly passed on can help, for it was as though my mother built a strengthening section to the bridge to make it that much easier to go across—if one can put it like that!

Minesta stated quite clearly in her introduction, and from her own personal experience, 'Those who have passed on come back from these realms of life [to communicate] because they love us'. She also speaks of what the newly-released soul will find on awaking in the other world: 'Those who on earth lived simply and loved others will quickly find companions in a world of exquisite beauty. They are also brought into contact with beings of greater spiritual power and enlightenment who will instruct them in the new ways of life'. In short, the principle of the life which continues, as well as the underlying pattern of earthly life, is *love*.

This is immensely reassuring, and I should like to end with a further, quite lengthy extract from that original preface because it demonstrates this love and the way in which each one of us can gently develop an understanding of and feeling for the little promptings we get from the other world.

'Try to conceive the heavenly state as being a perfect and harmonious outworking or expression of a law which is exact, but always expanding. Remember that you enter infinity when you are in the world of spirit.

'Let me try to illustrate this. In reply to a letter from a bereaved wife, I once wrote: "Your husband has come to me as this letter is being written. He wants you to know that there need be no separation between you even now, if you will only first use your imagination, and learn to think of him as alive and well, separated from you only because you fail to see him in his finer etheric body, which is at present outside your range of physical sight. This does not, however, preclude him from being with you in your home, and listening again with you to the music you formerly used to enjoy together. He himself continues, 'Although I do my best to make you see and feel me near you, as we are now functioning at different levels of life I find this impossible. I cannot so easily get down to you as you can get up to me. Through prayer and imagination try to conceive this higher state of life. So much for your waking hours; but when you fall asleep we can meet again, for you pass out of your body and I am waiting for you. Together we can then visit my home in the spirit life, or more correctly our home, because you are already a part of it. Indeed, we have created it together. But you do not remember these experiences when you wake up again to daily life. Nevertheless, you can train yourself to realize and remember that you belong to more worlds than one. You must try to get beyond the idea that dense physical matter is the only form which exists. There are many finer ethers, which form the substance of other spheres, many different degrees and states of life, each much more beautiful than the physical. You must learn to "dream true"; and you will do this by believing through your highest imagination in the state and condition of life in which I now find myself For it is here that all our high hopes and ideals are expressed in beauty and perfection—yes, in our spirit home, where I live permanently and where you occasionally visit me. In fact, this home is a manifestation of all our former hopes and dreams, which are becoming manifested or externalized in our surroundings."'

'The wife's letter of reply was impressive. In it she said their great mutual interest had been listening to fine music. They had both found great happiness in the creation of their home and garden. She said her husband had been both artistic and idealistic, and she could well understand why this "heaven" would take the form he had described. Nevertheless she herself was still in a "state of darkness" and felt desperately lonely. I pointed out that in fact she could only find her heaven within her own soul; that she must overcome self-pity, and let her thoughts dwell upon her husband's happiness rather than her own unhappiness; that she must try to think of him as he was now, and of the home that he had described. Then, I wrote, "You will gradually find the thick dark veil which at present seems impenetrable will become thinner, and you will know for certain that you are united in spirit. Afterwards you will quite simply and naturally find yourself with him when you wish to do so, in this other world which you two have built up. But remember also that you have your life and duties here on earth, which must not be neglected. You have to realize that nothing comes into being without its being first thought out in form, either in this world or the next. The whole creation is a product of God's thought."

'After a few weeks I received another letter from her. She was so changed, so full of joy because at last the darkness was dispersing, and she was beginning to get glimpses of the spiritual light. Her husband was using his own method of penetrating her consciousness. This was why she now felt so differently and was convinced that he was very close to her at times. Moreover, she was now waking in the morning with fleeting memories of a heaven world; and on occasions during the day he managed by devious means to signify his presence in the room; and the methods chosen were characteristic and convincing.'

We hope that today, even though it is many years since this book was first compiled, you the reader will still be able to draw great comfort and encouragement from White Eagle's pages about the higher and greater life.

July 2001

BIBLICAL REFERENCES AND
A NOTE ON THE SECOND EDITION

In response to reader requests, we offer below references for sayings of Jesus quoted from the Gospels, and other biblical references. For some readers other terms, such as 'Elder Brethren', could usefully be glossed. However, we would recommend a reader in search of definitions to turn to the latest White Eagle book, THE LIGHT BRINGER, pp. xiii–xv, where there are some useful notes. Our editorial policy is to avoid gender-specific language wherever possible, but to retain it where there is no convincing alternative, e.g. with the words 'brotherhood' and 'brethren'.

Page 21   the storm on the Sea of Galilee: Mt 8
Page 23   *that ye love one another:* Jn 15 : 12, 17
Page 23   *the fulfilling of the law:* Rom 13 : 10
Page 24   *he that believeth* on me: Jn 14 : 12
Page 25   the Transfiguration: Mt 17; Lk 9
Page 25   the Resurrection: see especially Jn 20, 21
Page 41   *seek ye first the Kingdom:* Mt 6 : 33
Page 52   *by their fruits:* Mt 7 : 20
Page 57   *the way, the truth, the life:* Jn 14 : 6
Page 59   Salvation: there are references to salvation by Christ in Lk 1, 2, and elsewhere. We would also recommend the useful discussion of the subject in two sections of White Eagle's book JESUS TEACHER AND HEALER, pp. 144–52
Page 59   the Comforter: loosely, from Jn 14

I: The Way, The Truth

WE THINK that fear of death, fear of transition from mortal to spiritual life, looms up for most people as the greatest bogey facing them; and, the more this apprehension seems to increase, the more developed the sensitive nervous system is in each person. By contrast, some of you can tranquilly say that for you all fear of death has passed. You can look through the thinning veil into the larger spiritual existence with complete confidence and indeed with happy anticipation; and can rejoice instead of grieving when one of your number has been visited by the great and compassionate Mother, called by some the Angel of Death, who comes at the appointed time to unbar the door between this world and the next. You think also of the joy with which your loved one goes forth into a sunlit garden as the door is flung wide. When you can truly rejoice at this liberation, you have indeed taken a great step forward.

It will help you if you can realize that there are two aspects of life: the first is the outer aspect in which you usually dwell; and the second, the inner or spiritual life which only comparatively few understand and live. The average person lives mostly a bodily life, sometimes for a number of incarnations, in a world which appears wholly material. Only occasionally does he or she become so shaken by sorrow or trouble as to reach out towards that other world. Usually, when all is going well, the average person is content. Today, we hope, an increasing number of people are awakening to the realization of the spiritual life.

Let us consider this inner world of which we speak. To some of you it may appear to be a purely mental world, because you find it by withdrawing from the outer, physical life into an inner state where it seems that you are living *in your mind*. You are often told that when you pass over you will live in a world of thought. You will find, however, that it is not only a world of thought, but also of feeling. Thought is at the next level to the physical; as you penetrate behind thought you come to a world of feeling and emotion.

You all live in this world of emotion, and your emotional life is also affected by the mental world around you, by the thoughts of others.

The recognition and control of your own body of feeling and emotion is one of the very first lessons to be learnt, if you would develop spiritual insight, because your feelings, if uncontrolled, are going to cause a storm. Do you remember the story of the disciples on the Sea of Galilee? As their Master slept in the boat beside them, a great storm arose, and in their fear they called upon the Master, who rose up in the boat and commanded the waters to be still and the storm to subside. The boat is a symbol of the soul;* the water, of the emotions; and the Master is the Christ, the spirit within, which alone can control the storms of emotion. You see from this that to protect yourself from adverse and disturbing thoughts, and to control your emotional body, you too must seek the love of God, the love of Christ. You must pray for, and strive to become, this gentle love.

The Inner Worlds are Substantial

Every human being is made up of substances identical with those of other spheres of life. We do not speak only of the physical body; remember you have other finer bodies, and each one of these is composed of

* In this context White Eagle means, by the soul, *being* itself. It is the 'ourself' of feelings, likes, dislikes, interests, affections, memories, sentiments—or to be more precise, the ourself which lives inside the outer being, and looks out through human eyes, speaks with the physical tongue and lips and thinks with the physical brain. It is this 'ourself' which survives death and migrates to a brighter realm.

the same substance as the plane upon which it functions. The planets around the earth are inhabited by beings made of the same substance as the planet on which they live. Accordingly sun-spirits or sun-beings can and do live on the sun, their bodies being composed of the substance of the sun. In the same way you have your own higher or finer bodies composed of substances identical with those of the higher worlds upon which they function. As you attain mastery over desire and emotion, you will learn to control and use these other bodies, and to contact the higher or inner worlds.

Violent emotions are as destructive to the higher bodies as the pure, lovely emotions are constructive; for the latter contain the creative power of God, while violent emotions contain the destructive power. This is the reason why we stress the necessity for control of your emotions as the first step towards conscious contact with the inner worlds.

Through prayer and meditation we may go deeper into this inner world of infinite love, infinite beauty. When a soul passes out of the body, by degrees it rises through the lower planes into the heavenly worlds—worlds of infinitely finer substance than this earth, yet as solid to those who inhabit them as your world seems to you. The people in these worlds of radiant colour and perfect form commune with each other harmoniously. They have work to do but their work is steady, quiet, serene. This is a world of love, God's world. This is heaven. When the soul arrives there it is conscious of one mighty realization, and that is of God, of the presence of the God of love, everywhere. Although it is not easy to do so, you yourself can reach this world if you will, while still on earth. During deep meditation, for instance, you may become aware of surpassing peace and harmony, of becoming raised in consciousness far beyond this world of space and time. You are then *en rapport* with heaven. To that heavenly life, all loving souls, the ordinary people of this earth, rise after death; but not always immediately. They have to pass through certain stages even as you have to undergo tests in your daily life.

The Transfiguration and Resurrection

It has often been noted that the Gospels say little about life after death, about a 'here' and a 'hereafter'. Jesus strove rather to convey that all truth is contained within one simple word: Love. Jesus said, *Love one another,* and St Paul went on to say, *Love is the fulfilling of the law'.*

Jesus was not wholly concerned with the spirit world; nor yet with the physical, intellectual, or emotional aspects of the human being. He did not divide life into segments, but considered human existence as a whole. He had learned the secrets of the perfect life, and the secret of control over all aspects of himself. In him there was no separation, for the Christ within him had revealed the whole of universal life. There was no need for him to speak about 'here' and 'hereafter' when to him death did not exist and life was eternal.

If each individual is to attain liberation from mortal bondage, then each must learn to practise and live the teaching of the Christ. Jesus, having perfected his physical vehicle and gained complete self-mastery, became a perfect vessel for the manifestation of the Christ; and he stated, *He that believeth on me, the works that I do shall he do also.* Few people try to practise the Presence of Christ; yet the joys of this heavenly life must be brought forth. As you truly long in your heart to reach that heavenly state you attract to your soul, to your life, the light of the Golden One, the very Christ being. As this light comes to you, you find truth deep within your heart, and your outer life begins to change, for you cannot live an untruth. The process of re-creation has begun; you have started on the upward arc towards heaven.

Perhaps you will now begin to understand why Jesus did not talk much about life after death, knowing that if his disciples put into operation the law which he had revealed, there was no need to speak of life after death, because death would be overcome. He demonstrated this in two ways; first by the Transfiguration, when he took three of his disciples up into the hills, or in other words raised their consciousness, and bade them watch with him, so that they saw the true life manifesting. Not only were they able to see the light of love blazing through his flesh, but in that light they saw the forms of other spiritual beings. They saw Jesus irradiated by the glory of the Christ, the Golden One.

In the Resurrection, Jesus provided the supreme example of the power of the Christ Spirit to transmute the earthly atoms to a higher form. The spirit of God, the Son of God, the Christ, had lived in full possession of the body of Jesus, and had so purified and transformed the physical atoms of that body that it became light, all light, as all physical bodies do when the light of Christ dwells in them. Illumined, they become this light. Light is another word for life, that is all. Life is God. The atoms of the body of Jesus were transformed into light, and disappeared from mortal vision. Yet it was still the same body. When your heart is cleansed by the Christ light your vision will open and heaven will be revealed to you. True love operating from within will enable you to know truth, to see through life and death to the hereafter.

II: Continuous Life

WE ARE SOMETIMES asked what life in the spirit world is really like. My friends, if you journeyed to another continent and later tried to describe that continent, you would find that words conveyed so little. Moreover, after a while your listener would get tired of your descriptions. The experiences of each newly-arrived soul in the beyond are individual according to the environment, character, and reactions of that soul. Therefore, what might bring profound joy to one soul might prove only boredom to another. So we can only answer you in this way: that life in the spirit world is very similar to life here on earth, except that the matter which forms the spirit world is not so dense or solid, and is more malleable than earth matter; while the spirit world (which is far closer to the physical than we realize) appears as solid to its inhabitants as earth does to you. Nevertheless, all its life and substance has a higher frequency or quicker vibration than this physical world.

The first thing a person wakes to after death is a world of his or her own creation. If that person has lived selfishly the people around him or her will be selfish, for like attracts like. People who have lived only to worship Mammon or riches will find themselves very poor afterwards, in very poverty-stricken surroundings. Having little spiritual substance in themselves, they will have little with which to build their home. Their environment will be a replica of their inner self, their self externalized.

The life that is lived on earth is being reflected over into the spirit life, but with a difference; because over there all that is ugly, crude and distasteful is more apparent, more difficult to disguise and conceal, and therefore intensified. So also with the more kindly, affectionate and refined life, which expresses itself in beauty, in art and science, and in harmony with humanity and nature. All these are also intensified, both in the person and his or her surroundings. Most spirit people are overcome with joy when they see the wondrous beauty of their world revealed, when they see the Godlike expressed through nature, art, music, science, healing, and in the angelic world. They find they are able to see the 'within' of life instead of only the surface as before. They see this inward life as an expression of all that is good and true and beautiful, an expression of God. We cannot describe the wonder and, above all, the freedom of the spirit world. Spirit people have only to think or wish to be in a certain place and they are there. They have only to create strongly in their minds a garden where exquisite flowers bloom, and they are within that garden. They have only to think, to long, hope or dream, and their thoughts or dreams become their realities.

Life after death offers richer and deeper joy and satisfaction, and greater opportunity than life on earth can ever give; because true aspiration brings opportunity to the soul immediately—whereas on earth you may dream and hope, but always seem to be limited by your environment and fate. In spirit you are freed. If you truly love God, if you are endeavouring to express the God within yourself, you find yourself in exactly the conditions to which your soul aspired, with opportunities to study, to work, or to research. All such creative joys are open to you.

You often wonder whether the spirit people eat. Why should they not eat? We certainly eat, not flesh of animals, but fruits that grow in the spirit world. Life in our world is perfectly natural. We are not yolkless, shell-less eggs! We are perfectly normal people with bodies and homes and gardens and all the things which we need. We live a perfectly natural, normal life. You think that we have no body, but you are wrong: we have etheric, astral and mental bodies, but you cannot see them. You too have other bodies, and the more evolved you become, the more you develop the higher bodies.

You can aspire to the higher worlds, and so can we. We are not limited to one plane. We live at a level of existence that we find restful and congenial, but there are higher levels to which we can aspire when we have learnt how to find them. Even we cannot live forever on the mountaintops, however. We cannot emphasize too strongly the naturalness and the beauty of our life. But remember that with you as with us, it is the quality of the consciousness of the soul which decides where the soul will find itself, either during the sleep state or after shedding the physical body.

All Worlds are One!

Contained within his physical body man has another body called the etheric, which merges into the physical just as water permeates a sponge. The etheric is closely related to the nervous system. Therefore it is this body which registers all sensations, pleasurable or otherwise. When it is driven out by, say, an anaesthetic, the physical body feels no pain. The etheric also forms a bridge across which spirits communicate. It possesses two parts: a higher which merges into the astral body after death, and a lower which is closely related to the physical. This part is known to linger about its former home; around buildings, fields, gardens; to cling to any place familiar to it, including churchyards; and is sometimes called a wraith or ghost. It is not the true self, only a counterpart, a semblance. What is known as a ghost is the etheric emanation left behind after the death of the body. This etheric emanation can be earthbound for a long time, but more usually disintegrates with the body.

Next we come to the astral body, which registers the emotions or feelings, and which also permeates the physical. You live even now in your etheric and astral bodies. It is in them that you feel pain or pleasure, or the emotions of love and hate, fear and hope—sensations and feelings of all kinds. The physical body is only clothing, an overcoat. When this is laid aside, you continue to live in your subtler bodies, just the same person, inhabiting just these same bodies—with nothing fearful and hardly anything strange to dread in the experience of death. Beyond the astral planes (which may be thought of as a series of 'earths' but of finer quality) are the mental planes inhabited by your mental bodies (which also are part of you, here and now). We now come closer to the higher self, or the angelic or heavenly body, most beautiful in appearance and shining with a great light. Every human being has such a body, though undeveloped; but it evolves during various lives (many, many lives indeed), and is in reality the temple of the spirit.

In these celestial realms dwell the angelic hierarchies, along with the saints and perfected souls of all ages; indeed, all souls dwell here who have passed through great tribulation in this world and so become harmonized with the divine Law of Love.

We can hear some of you saying, 'All we want is to continue the same sort of life as this, and not to soar away to some vague heaven. Let us keep ourselves safely tethered to familiar things and we shall be happy'.

Subconsciously, however, most of you long for a better world. You feel in some way attached to this life of spirit—and rightly so, for it is your true home. You have come from this world of spirit to live in the flesh, where you are imprisoned until you learn to free yourself. Intuition tells you that you come from a more beautiful place than this earth, for a purpose and according to a plan, and that the great Architect, the Creator of the Universe, holds the plan of all your lives. You are like children who have come back to school; and your own soul, although its memory has faded for the time being, subconsciously knows that you have come here to be trained to gain certain knowledge. Your daily life which seems so irksome, your body which is so tiresome to maintain: in reality they are the restrictions which quicken your soul, and help you to unfold the soul qualities which must be developed before you can be free from the bondage of physical life. We do not mean freedom through death, because death does not necessarily set you free from bondage. You can only free yourself from the limitations of the lower self by your own efforts. Once you have freed yourself you may enter into the heaven world of peace and serenity, of beauty, of joy.

You may ask who can best help you during this long pilgrimage. We answer that you have one particular teacher or guide, who may be attached to you through a number of lives. You will also have a number of helpers, who come to help you through some particular period; sometimes these are also called guides, but in error. If you will try to listen to your guide, who comes on a higher level than the helpers, he or she will speak through the voice of your higher self (which sometimes you hear as your conscience) or, as it is sometimes called, the voice of God.

It is a true saying that everything comes right in the end, that it must and does come right. Why then be fearful? You can experience many troubles and still keep happy. It all depends on how you take them. If you surrender to the will of God, you will find inward happiness, unbelievable joy. You will always get wonderful, kindly and gentle help from those who are invisible. Always ready, they love to do something which brings you blessing and compensation. So, although you may have to learn lessons through hard knocks, you will also receive compensation, service and blessing from the unseen.

They do not forget, and would come to help you, but can only descend so far. All is a matter of vibration, harmony, attunement. Earth is of a slow vibration. You mortal beings must quicken, and become attuned. You must raise yourselves to meet and greet your spirit friends. It is all so simple, so clear—and yet, so profound, so difficult to attain. In spirit as on earth, only 'keeping on keeping on' will get you anywhere.

Pray that you may learn to free yourself from the thraldom of the lower bodily self, and enter into the heaven world of peace and serenity, beauty and joy, and hold sweet and true communion with these higher worlds and reap their blessing.

The Means to Reach Heaven

A powerful means of contacting the heaven world is during sleep. As we have previously told you, many people already do this. You may say that your dreams are too confused, too muddled to be of value. Of course, there are various types of dream, many being due to bodily discomfort of some kind. But we have in mind a more real and vivid dream which leaves a deep impression afterwards—a vision, in fact, which usually comes in the early morning, on waking.

You should prepare for these sleep-experiences, and at the same time you will be preparing for the development of the spiritual faculties, the higher psychic powers. The first requirement, as we have said, is aspiration, which of necessity will mean prayer. You will pray, not necessarily with your lips but with your heart; you will reach upward to God, to the Father–Mother–Son, the holy and blessed Three, as you seek communion. We have said many times that those on earth must reach halfway at least if they would commune with spirit.

Next we would suggest that you practise breathing. We mean conscious breathing-in of the light, of the life of God; and the conscious breathing-out of love to all human kind.

'Breathe on me, Breath of God': so run the first words of the old hymn. Breathe in God. Breathe out God's love. Breathe out God's blessing to all human life. This deep rhythmic breathing does more than affect the body. Seen clairvoyantly, the person breathing in, in full consciousness of divine life, is strengthening his or her soul and causing it to radiate a great light. Instantly, by power of the Christ within, that person can send a shaft of light across the world, or up into spheres immeasurable. There need be no separation in spirit where there is the impetus of divine love.

One of the symbols used in the Greek and Egyptian Mysteries was a great winged disc, and another was the sphinx, whose wings indicate the power of the soul to fly. No restrictions hold down the individual spirit, unless they are self-made. Therefore think of yourself as having wings on your shoulders, as being encircled by a winged disc, symbolizing the sun or the Christ spirit. Within your heart is the golden sun, your spirit, which can rise on wings into realms supernal. All of you have the power so to fly, and must learn to use it.

So let aspiration come first, then prayer and correct breathing, and surrender to God. What is the next requisite? It is that you should learn to live daily a serene and tranquil life. We do not mean you should become too serious or solemn; if you do, you will chain yourself to the heaviness of the earth's atmosphere. Be very still and quiet, but also have the joy of the spirit singing within you and laughter on your lips. The Elder Brethren in spirit have a lively sense of humour, and love laughter.

We encourage happiness, a zest for living; but there is a time to be still, and that time is when you seek communion with a higher world and with visitors from that world. They come on a very fine and delicate vibration and work through the etheric body which is interlaced with your nervous system. Noise or discord breaks the fine contact.

Before you go to sleep, if you wish to make conscious contact with the spirit realms, do as we have suggested, but do not force yourself too hard. Take everything harmoniously. Within you is a power which we describe as 'divine will', and this can be the motive force which lifts you to divine realms. According to your soul's awareness, it will be taken to the place in the spirit world where it will find both its lesson and refreshment, and where it will rejoin its friends and companions in the sphere of reunion. Perhaps it will be taken to the Halls of Learning. These are immense buildings, with beautiful columns supporting a dome-shaped roof. The walls are rather like cinema screens which can reflect pictures of your own past lives and episodes which happened very long ago in the earth's history. You will at once want to know what good such visions can be to you? They serve to teach you, to stimulate your spirit, and to help you to bring back memories of the Ancient Wisdom which will help you in your future work; for what happened in the soul's past moulds its future.

We must now give a word of warning. Such work as this must never be undertaken with any selfish motive or to satisfy curiosity. This is dangerous. If you love others, you will want to develop spiritual powers primarily in order to serve them the better. Selfishness is a definite hindrance.

The keynote of your life is love and service; as you love and serve God and human kind, you will radiate the light. Before you lies a path of never-ending progress. Do not let the heaviness of the world hold you down, but go forward as a pilgrim on the path of spiritual unfoldment.

III: A Day for Remembering

TODAY* YOUR THOUGHTS centre upon those who laid
down their lives in two world wars. Many of you long
to know what happens to those killed in battle. My
friends, think of your body as an overcoat; then think
of that 'overcoat' as being shot through, or immersed
in water, or burned, and you will recognize that an
'overcoat' cannot feel or see. Neither did those who
died, because at that time they were not in their overcoat. At the appointed moment the spirit is withdrawn
from the physical body in a way which you cannot
understand. It is as though a veil is drawn across so that
the spirit is unconscious of the suffering of the body,
and death then becomes a beautiful experience, in
spite of what may appear. The heart may shrink from
the thought of pain and death beforehand, but when

*This talk was given on a national Day of Remembrance, such as
falls in the British Commonwealth of Nations in November, and
in the USA as Memorial Day, in May.

39

death actually comes, all fear goes. The soul is simply aware of great peace … aware of God.

Our words are borne out by multitudes. When the soul is in grave danger or when it faces death, you have many reminders of how it cries out to God instinctively and urgently. And God never fails. The actual moment of death is not felt or realized. Those who die in battle may be aware of the near approach of death, and then they find themselves out of their bodies. They may even see their stricken bodies fall—but no change takes place in themselves. Someone meets them and in a perfectly natural way takes them to a place where they may find rest and refreshment. All is natural, normal and happy, nor are they separated from their earthly relatives, who often visit them on falling asleep at night.

It is sad that the many people who mourn do not know what happens after death; they receive no message, have no feeling that their dear ones are close, have nothing left but saddening memories—or so they think. They misinterpret the message of the scriptures and mentally close down a shutter between the two worlds. Others believe that although a person survives death, he or she passes away forever from the earth. We have heard you say, 'My loved one has gone right away. I shall never find her in the spirit world'. 'He has been in spirit now for such a long time and must have progressed far beyond me.'

We want to help you to understand what really happens. Many, many times we have said that where there is true love, there is no separation; because in that love you are all united. At a certain soul-level 'communion of saints' becomes a very real thing.

Human souls are like drops in the ocean or grains of sand on the seashore. Each is individual, each a unit, but all can blend together to make one grand whole. Many people fear that when they reach a state of advanced spirituality, they will lose their identity in God, but this is a mistake. God has created you to be His–Her son or daughter, God's child for ever-more; of course you are always a part of God. But you have been given an individual spirit, so when you unite with the great family of God you are still individual and you will always retain your identity.

Try never to set material things before God-things. *Seek ye first the kingdom of God*. Let that kingdom become the main desire of your heart, your first aspiration on waking. Seek God and all the beauty of God's world. Then you will be living with a purpose. Then you will be progressing towards your ultimate goal, which is complete union with the Holy and Infinite Life, at-one-ment with the Father. But always you will remain yourself because God has endowed you with a personal life.

Nevertheless your bliss comes when you learn to

surrender self, when you recognize your at-one-ment with the whole, and thus are able to share in the communion of saints.

At special times, such as your Remembrance or Memorial Days, a whole host of souls come back in great power because the people of earth are thinking of them and are sending out their love to them again. Whenever the earth people pray, and so turn their thoughts to their loved ones, the way is opened for them to return. That is why at this time a great company of shining ones descends to bring to those they love something of the light and truth they themselves have found. We remind you, however, that you do not necessarily have to die before you too can pass freely into this higher world and see clearly the life of those who dwell therein.

We are now especially speaking to those who have lost someone near and dear to them. We say that they are just the same as when you formerly knew and loved them. They are the same personalities; they are still your own father or son, brother or sister, husband or wife. They are just the same, only so much happier because they are freed from the cares, distress and confusion of earth. Their joy increases when they feel you are attuned to them in your soul, and that you believe and know that they are close. Try to talk to them within your soul body, mentally, and make them real to you.

We tell you with tenderness that you bring much of your suffering upon yourselves. You will ask how we can say this when, for instance, your hearts are sore through bereavement. No, of course you did not bring bereavement upon yourself—only the suffering which resulted from your attitude of mind. For if you had developed power to penetrate the mists of earthliness, you would have known that your dear one was not dead or far away. Communion of soul with soul is always waiting for the man or woman who can develop, within, a consciousness of the oneness of all life. Learn so to love God that you know that God, being all love, and having all love for you, has in Him–Her no death, but only a more abundant life. Your loved one dwells within that Love, and also within your own spirit. Your loved one is therefore with you, not lost, not gone far away.

Try never to think of anyone as being 'dead'. Think of them as living more abundantly in a land which you know they would love—and please, not as living idly; idleness they would not find inspiring. Wherever their heart inclines them they will find their work, and work to their heart's content.

Believe that all the experiences of your daily life come to discipline and to teach you, even if they are sometimes painful; for joy only comes about through pain. The wise person knows that even when apparent tragedy brings bereavement to a family, it is presently revealed to them that a wise purpose has been served, in that the passing brought an eventual fulfilment to many people.

The wise one never grieves over the dead or over the living, because he or she knows that God in His–Her wisdom and compassion cares for and succours all earthly creatures. How can we ever find adequate words truly to convey to the anxious human heart the rich love, the transcendent beauty, and the enduring peace of God?

IV: True Communion

Children in Spirit Life

WHAT HAPPENS to a baby or little child when it passes on? It must be remembered that only from the physical viewpoint does the child seem to die. An angel of death is present at the moment of transition, so that the soul falls into a deep sleep, and in angelic care is tenderly and lovingly borne away. The child awakens in the spirit world with the spirit of the Divine Mother at its side. Her sweet influence enfolds the child and calms its every fear.

Provision will have been made in advance for the child's particular temperamental needs. Often some loved relative, perhaps a grandmother (or even its own mother, who may be sleeping at the time) will be brought, and replicas of favourite toys will claim its attention.

Children who pass on do not suffer any sense of

physical loss, for having been absent from the spirit for only a short period they are still at home there. To them it is like returning to a place they remember and love, although the memory of their newly-acquired earth parents is still retained. They quickly enjoy all that is provided to make them happy. They live in homes set in a lovely countryside, enjoy games, and have other forms of recreation; when old enough they attend schools, or places of learning. Everywhere they go is permeated with a feeling that the Divine Love is present and they are safe. The children happily explore and become familiar with their world of nature, and make friends with the 'fairy' folk which abound there—the nature spirits—as well as with the many other children who come over from the earth life.

Moreover, they are still on familiar terms with their parents, and meet them many times when the latter are set free during sleep. The parents afterwards forget their dream of reunion, and cannot recall the homes they visited, set in the country or by lake or sea.

The children grow quickly over there. Time in spirit cannot be compared with human time. Those who lose a loved daughter or dear son by death can rest assured that all is well with the one they have lost; and that when their own time comes to pass over they will be reunited with the child. For a period only, the child will regain the appearance which they remember, so that there will be no strangeness when they meet.

The life beyond would be incomplete without the companionship of animals. These too survive death; they too enjoy a life of freedom with all the joys of their animal life, except that they do not hunt or kill. For them their new life is a replica of their old, but made just, perfect and beautiful in every detail. Nevertheless, they remember their former friends and human companions, and await their coming in the heaven world.

Real Evidence and Truth

To those who require proof, we can only repeat what we once said to a man who asked us to convince him that humans survived death. We asked our questioner to give decisive proof that there is *no* life after death. He failed, for no one can disprove this fact. But on the other hand many thousands, perhaps millions, have received direct evidence of life beyond the grave. Yet proof cannot come through any one episode or isolated fact; indeed we might produce remarkable psychic phenomena at this instant, but these would not necessarily prove that your own personal life will continue beyond the grave.

Truth is a revelation of the God within your own being. The only real and lasting proof of immortality comes as a revelation to your innermost spirit, and is not dependent upon outward things. When this inner revelation comes, you are assured that certain things are unshakeably true; but if you were challenged to prove them to others you would find it very difficult to do so. You can prove them to your own inner satisfaction, because the God within you knows truth. Similarly, the God in everyone should recognize truth or God in his or her brother or sister.

Therefore, to those who demand proof of a life after death, we say: *follow the light within your own breast.* Seek revelation, and as surely as night follows day, you will accumulate experiences which will be absolute proof to you of a life beyond this earthly one.

Communication and Communion

You will want to know whether it is possible for a discarnate soul to communicate through a medium? Yes, true communications can and do come in this way, but it is a somewhat uncertain method of communication because perfect conditions are hard to come by. Nevertheless it can help and comfort people on both sides of the veil, more especially soon after a passing, and must not be condemned as undesirable or wrong.

May we suggest the importance of quickening all your perceptions when you are hoping to receive messages from the world of spirit through a medium?

We have sometimes been sad to witness the efforts made by the spirit people to reach someone who was rather dull in understanding. We know that you say, 'Oh, we like to have all our 't's crossed and the 'i's dotted.' But those in spirit do not always cross the 't's and dot the 'i's, not because they decline to satisfy your reasoning mind, but because they want you to use your own God-given gifts. They want you to do some of the work yourself. Communication is like a bridge reaching from one world to the other. There must be an effort from both sides for a meeting to take place. So remember that you are as much responsible for building your part of the bridge as your communicators are for their part.

As we have said, communication from our side of life to yours travels via the etheric body. The etheric body is connected with, indeed interpenetrates, the nervous system. A medium is usually a highly-strung and sensitive instrument, so that when communication is being sought, his or her whole nervous organism becomes keyed up.

People have attempted to devise a physical instrument which will serve as a bridge, and thus eliminate the medium. They think that communications received in this way would be much more reliable. We do not think this is correct. We think that communication between the two worlds will always depend to a degree upon the ultra-sensitive human organism.

What we will call 'outer' communication through a medium can take many forms, such as clairvoyance, psychometry, direct voice, and automatic writing. But although many true and good communications can and have come through in this way, remember that the messages received do not necessarily always come from the spirit. They can come from the subconscious mind, or in the case of some clairvoyance and in psychometry can be a form of 'aura reading'. We do not say that it is impossible for true and clear messages to come through, but you must remember the many factors which can make this form of communication unreliable.* Sometimes a message will come through perfectly clearly; another time it will be confused and hazy. It is necessary for the medium to have certain qualifications; for instance the power to become attuned to God, to resign mind and heart to the supreme truth, wisdom and love of the Great White Spirit. We emphasize that the medium must concentrate wholly upon and wholly desire truth, eliminating all self-desire; and this is not easy for the ordinary person.

We still think, therefore, that the safer and wiser path is to unfold your own spiritual faculties—we do not mean psychic gifts—and thereby to reach up so that you yourself can commune with the beyond. A message, a

*The reader who wishes to study further the subject of mediumistic gifts is recommended to another White Eagle book, SPIRITUAL UNFOLDMENT ONE (second edition, 2001).

feeling, a conviction right in the heart that your dear one has spoken direct to you means more than numerous psychic evidences; for beyond all these outer methods of communication via the etheric body is what we are going to call communion of spirit. When you touch this plane you are nearing contact with pure truth, for communion does not come via any of the psychic senses, but in the heart chakra. You perhaps know where the heart chakra is. To the clairvoyant it looks like a disc of light over the heart. In one who is unawakened it glows so that it is just visible, but in the spiritually-quickened it is pure, beautiful and radiant. The pictures of the saints sometimes depict a jewel blazing on the breast. Our Roman Catholic brothers and sisters draw attention to the heart chakra by the flaming heart seen in pictures of the Master Jesus. Through this radiation and development communion is able to take place.

In this kind of communion no words are needed. Shall we call it the language of the heart? The recipient of the message from the spirit has an inner knowing, a certainty. Sometimes with a medium you may listen to messages which are meant to direct your mind along certain channels; these messages will attune you to a spiritual plane of consciousness where you will receive an inner knowing. You may not be able to explain its nature to any living soul afterwards. Nevertheless you will feel an absolute certainty that you have been holding communion with one who is very near and dear. For this you do not need words. There has been an interplay, an inflow of spiritual light from heart to heart, an affinity, an attunement of spirit. You have indeed experienced true communion.

Usually this vital inner communication with the beyond comes to those who have prepared themselves. You need not necessarily seek to be alone in a church or sanctuary; you may unconsciously raise yourself through prayer. Your prayer may be unuttered yet a true prayer to God. The very act of prayer truly attunes a man or woman to the world of spirit.

You should of course be well-balanced and sensible about these things. You must live on earth in the right way, understanding that you are here in a body for a certain purpose. This communication from the world of pure spirit will not be denied if you keep humble in heart and simple in faith and trustful in the eternal love. If you hear something which seems Godlike, true and beautiful in its wisdom, do not say afterwards, 'It was all my imagination'. No visitor from a realm above will give a message contrary to the law of Christ, nor speak words which are unkind or hurtful; and will never send you off on some wild-goose chase. *By their fruits ye shall know them.* What comes from the Christ circle will bear its stamp or hallmark.

The condition, then, for clear and perfect reception is one of stillness of mind and silence; not only on the outer plane but deep, deep, deep within the inner world, the inner place. Beyond all conflicting vibrations is the Silence; and in that Silence is God. God is behind all form, all activity, all manifestation.

This centre of light within your own being is not confined to you alone, for as it unfolds it reaches out and touches the Universal. Then you will become *en rapport* with radiant beings whom you love to contact. Remember that your own loved ones, after passing through the astral planes, go onward and become conscious of the celestial world, and in that celestial world you can meet them face to face. Never make the mistake of thinking that because you dwell in a body you are bound down to the material world only and are ruled by material things. You are divine as well as human. Remember you have a celestial body as well as a physical, which has been given you to use even now. It is a great error to believe that you cannot reach the glories of the heaven world. In the course of your evolution, you will have to learn how to go as a traveller, a visitor, to your true home in the celestial world, and there see for yourself the glories which are prepared for every soul who loves God.

The place of communion is the temple within your own being of which the Master Jesus spoke; which all Masters through all ages have taught their pupils to seek, a communion in which you eat the bread and drink the wine of life. The Holy Grail is within your heart; it is also the Universal Cup. Pursue your path patiently; you will surely reach your goal and know the joy of life, for all the mists will clear and happiness will be your crown.

v: The Temple of Light

WHILE YOU ARE here on earth you are building a temple. In the first place you are maintaining your body by the kind of food you eat, the air you breathe. The desires, emotions, tastes of earthly life are simultaneously building your astral body; and your thoughts, your imagination, your prayer, your aspiration and all the instincts of your creative self are building your higher mental body. To an advanced clairvoyant all these bodies are visible in the aura. The astral body which pervades and surrounds the physical is seen as an emanation of colour: either refined and delicate or coarse, crude and ugly. The more highly evolved and sensitive the person, the more beautiful the aura becomes. To be seen interpenetrating the astral is the radiation of the mental body; and there are several higher auras which are more rarely seen.

You must develop special senses, and pure and subtle bodies, in order to reach and penetrate the pure and subtle planes of life. But if you neither think about nor aspire to a higher life, if you are content with cruder material things, you cannot hope to get there. Truly to contact the higher planes of life the body must be purified by right living, right aspiration, true prayer and a constant reaching upward. The astral body is contacted by means of heavenly desires, by spiritual aspiration, by refined tastes, and love of beauty in all its forms; the mental body by meditation, imagination, a continual reaching up, as we say. Thus you are building and perfecting your subtler bodies; but until you have developed them, you are living in a kind of prison house.

Beyond the mental plane is what we call 'the Temple of Light'. It is from that level that the soul eventually returns to incarnation, but it can dwell there in a state of supreme happiness and bliss for a long time after its strenuous years of service on earth. There is no hard-and-fast rule as to how long this shall be. There is no forcing of a soul back into incarnation, although it is the law of life that it shall eventually come back. At a certain stage of its spiritual evolution the soul quickens—awakens, as it were—and itself decides to retrace its steps and reincarnate, not only to gain more knowledge but often to give wider and greater service.

All that the soul ever performs and experiences on the earth is being built into its Temple of Light. Through spiritual training and development alone you can become aware of your Temple, or your celestial body, while still on earth. When, in your meditation, you are caught up into a pure and glorious state of consciousness, you touch your celestial body.

The human soul is comprised of the astral and mental bodies and the celestial body or 'Temple of Light' of which we have just spoken. These comprise the soul; but there is something else; there is the individual spirit. When the soul has perfected itself—that is—has garnered all the experience possible from the physical life, the spirit is ready to undergo the Christ initiation. A wonderful 'resurrection' or enlightenment is waiting when the Christ in man–woman, or the spirit within, stirs and awakens. Christ himself paved the way for this quickening of humanity; and Jesus became the Christed One who trod the path and demonstrated the way to humanity. He said, *I am the way, the truth and the life*—the way to life eternal.

Some people think that humanity cannot save itself without worshipping Jesus Christ who was crucified on the cross. This is not so. It is not the outer Christ that human kind is seeking, except as an example and demonstration. Each person's great need is to find the inner Christ.

Thus, when the Temple of Light is completed,

there comes rebirth into heavenly conditions, birth into a life of pure bliss.

The Christ Consciousness

How can you as an individual bring into your life the power and the life of the Cosmic Christ? First, by remembering that Christ is not some remote being whom you meet some day, if you are good enough, after you have passed away from the earth. No, Christ is an ever-present power and intelligence, Christ is a friend, a brother to you now, if you so wish; he–she is also a saviour. We are not speaking so much of the human Master Jesus, but of the cosmic and mystical glory which has been since the beginning of life on this planet; and yet which is so understanding of humanity's needs that it can and does take upon itself human form. It is very important for you to realize that this being of light and glory can come to you in a human form, understanding human and personal problems, understanding your perplexity, your fears, your grief, your loneliness.

Today men and women have developed mentally, but lacking wisdom they have neither the humility nor the simplicity in their hearts to enable them to comprehend the beauty and the glory of the Creator's love. If some day you think you have seen a vision of the Master Jesus, this is not mere imagination. Jesus also is not separate from humanity. His soul was prepared for his great mission, and he was sent forth by his Creator to this earth to be used by Christ, the Son of God, so that Christ could speak through a human personality to tell all people the truth about their salvation.

For 'salvation' is the right and only word to describe the mission of the Christ Spirit; for when the Christ Spirit quickens in a man or a woman, that person is literally *saved* from their sins. There is no attachment to the things of this world, once the Christ Spirit quickens within and the person has grown to full stature. This is the meaning of 'salvation for all humanity'—not salvation through a person's belief in one particular man, but salvation by reason of the Christ love within each person, each individual self. This will forbid anyone to wage war or to treat others as less than than they. The Christ love will inspire all men and women to words and actions of kindness and consideration—to work for God in daily life; to live in consciousness of a glory above, around and within. This is salvation by Christ.

Jesus once said to his disciples and to those who had ears to hear, and minds and hearts ready for the truth: *Lo, I will send you a Comforter.* He said also, *If I do not go from you*—if I do not leave you—*you will not know the Comforter.* Your Comforter, my children, is the Christ within. Christ comes to bring to you illumination, a vision of the glory of the whole plan of human creation.

Are you bereaved, my brother, my sister? Have you lost one who is near and dear to you, and are you yearning, searching on the outer, the physical plane, for that lost one? You feel that the heavens are as brass and you make no contact. Rise through earnest prayer direct to Christ as one who knows and understands your sorrow and your need; then the heavens will open and the Comforter will come into your heart, your vision will clear and you will see your loved one. Then you will know that where you love you cannot lose; for when you love, you are united in love; there is no separation.

If you are sick, and are faced perhaps with a long illness, or the illness of one you love, you can still rise in your spirit to meet Christ, the Golden One. When you can truly do this, all sickness and pain are healed. Christ is the great healer; the power was demonstrated through Jesus, who is still today demonstrating the healing power of the Creator. You need to put aside childish, earthly things, and live in the consciousness of an enfolding, interpenetrating life-power which is all love and wisdom.

Are you anxious about tomorrow? Can you see no way to turn? Do you fear to take the next step? Turn, then, to the Golden One; be patient and rest in faith: in more than faith—in full consciousness of

God's wisdom. You have no need to be anxious or to fear. Your Creator loves you and is guiding you step by step. Formerly you have tried this path and that, and they reach nowhere. But at last, as you rise in spirit towards the Golden One, you come again to the main stream, which is your life, and that life is now leading you directly home. You must know that this guiding light and love are ever with you; through life and through the great initiation called death it will never leave you.

So, children of earth, we raise your consciousness again to the Christ Life which is all love, wisdom and strength. Be still and lift up your hearts as children in simplicity. See for yourselves the glory of the arisen Christ. You are in the company of heaven. Hosts and hosts of shining forms surround you. Silently commune with this vast company and with the King of Kings, your Saviour....

Take heart, have courage. Begin afresh from this very moment to do all good, and to love with all your heart and to be thankful for every blessing of your daily lives. Know always that underneath are the everlasting arms, in this world and in all worlds to come.

Other books in the
'Your Journey in the Light' series

The present book is one of a series of handy anthologies of White Eagle's teaching. All these books contain passages for meditation and study, short enough to read one section at a time, perhaps before bed or as a daily inspiration. White Eagle's words go unfailingly where our need is—or directly to the heart.

HEAL THYSELF

A way for everyone, sick or well, to find and retain true health in mind and body.

New edition, ISBN 0-85487-107-1.

MORNING LIGHT

A guide to anyone who is setting out upon a spiritual path. White Eagle's words of love encourage every man or woman who recognizes something of the true nature of their being and seeks to bring that knowledge of the God within into expression in the physical life.

Subjects covered include the finding of the inner turth, mriacles, the Christ- or sun-power, the illusory character of separation, the Brotherhood in spirit, worship, service, and the way to rise in meditation into the golden world of spirit.

'Light radiates from the pages.' SCIENCE OF THOUGHT REVIEW. ISBN 0-85487-115-2.

GOLDEN HARVEST

The man or woman who enters into their own kingdom—the kingdom of true consciousness—is a supremely happy being. The words of White Eagle which have been chosen to make up this book take us to the centre of love in our own hearts, and when we touch this magic place of light all the viscissitudes and irritations of life fall away as things that are un-important or illusory. The reward, then, of discovering and holding to the true consciousness—the consciousness of love—is a true golden harvest.

This is one of the most popular and loved of all White Eagle's books and forms a natural sequel to MORNING LIGHT, the introductory book of the series.

New edition, ISBN 0-85487-106-9

THE GENTLE BROTHER

White Eagle's gentle yet uncompromising words spoken to his wide 'family' for their everyday help and guidance. In this much-loved book, a classic of his teaching, they are collected in the form of short extracts to be used as day-to-day reading or to turn to in times of need.

A reader wrote: 'Of all the basic books of White Eagle's teaching, THE GENTLE BROTHER has most been a spiritual friend and companion for me—warm, light and profound'.

New edition, ISBN 0-85487-112-8.